MW00947817

# Fourth Grade Writing Prompts for Seasons:
# A Creative Writing Workbook

Bryan Cohen

This publication is protected under the US Copyright Act of 1976 and all other applicable international, federal, state and local laws, and all rights are reserved, including resale rights: you are not allowed to give or sell this book to anyone else. If you received this publication from anyone other than Bryan Cohen, Amazon or Build Creative Writing Ideas, you've received a pirated copy. Please contact us via the website and notify us of the situation.

All contents Copyright © 2012 by Build Creative Writing Ideas and Bryan Cohen. All rights reserved. No part of this document or the related files may be reproduced or transmitted in any form, by any means (electronic, photocopying, recording, or otherwise) without the prior written permission of the publisher.

Limit of Liability and Disclaimer of Warranty: The publisher has used its best efforts in preparing this book, and the information provided herein is provided "as is." Bryan Cohen and Build Creative Writing Ideas make no representation or warranties with respect to the accuracy or completeness of the contents of this book and specifically disclaims any implied warranties of merchantability or fitness for any particular purpose and shall in no event be liable for any loss of profit or any other commercial damage, including but not limited to special, incidental, consequential, or other damages. All characters appearing in this work are fictitious. Any resemblance to real persons, living or dead, is purely coincidental.

Trademarks: This book identifies product names and services known to be trademarks, registered trademarks, or service marks of their respective holders. They are used throughout this book in an editorial fashion only. In addition, terms suspected of being trademarks, registered trademarks, or service marks have been appropriately capitalized, although Bryan Cohen and Build Creative Writing Ideas cannot attest to the accuracy of this information. Use of a term in this book should not be regarded as affecting the validity of any trademark, registered trademark, or service mark. Bryan Cohen and Build Creative Writing Ideas are not associated with any product or vendor mentioned in this book.

Finally, use your head. Nothing in this book is intended to replace common sense, legal, medical or other professional advice, and is meant to inform and entertain the reader. So have fun with the book and happy writing!

Edited by Ashley Daoust.

Copyright © 2012 Build Creative Writing Ideas and Bryan Cohen

All rights reserved.

ISBN: 1479382329
ISBN-13: 978-1479382323

## DEDICATION

I dedicate this book to Dr. Mark Obenrader, my childhood doctor, who made sure that my five senses were in tip top shape for all four seasons.

# CONTENTS

# INTRODUCTION

Welcome to the *Writing Prompts for Seasons* workbook series! Within these pages you'll find 200 writing prompts, two on each page, that will stimulate the imagination of your students or children. I've found that the key to allowing students to fully latch onto an idea is to give them a scenario followed by a question. In answering the question, young writers can take the same prompt a million different directions. You may even want to try photocopying a page and have your writers take on the same prompt at the beginning and the end of a school year, just to see how different their storytelling has become.

The *Writing Prompts for Seasons* series is a collection of books I've created after seeing how many parents and teachers have visited my website, Build Creative Writing Ideas (located at http://www.build-creative-writing-ideas.com). The most popular pages on my site coincide with prompts about the four seasons of spring, summer, fall and winter. I imagine this means two things: teachers and parents are searching for seasonal writing activities, and children enjoy writing about the changing weather and the upcoming holidays. I hope that this series will meet both of those needs while inspiring creativity in the minds of our youth. The five books in the series are available for grades 1, 2, 3, 4 and 5. The prompts become more complex with each volume, but continue to remain imaginative and creative throughout.

I love hearing about the progress of students on my site and I'm always interested in hearing new ideas for delivering creative writing prompts to writers from the ages of 5 to 105. Feel free to contact me on my website with any questions and comments you can think of. I hope you and your future best-selling authors thoroughly enjoy this and other books in the series. Happy writing!

Sincerely,
Bryan Cohen
Author of *Writing Prompts for Seasons*

PS: While there is space below each prompt for your budding writers to write, there is a good chance they may have more to say than they can fit on the page. There is an extra page in the back if you'd like to photocopy it, but I strongly suggest that you also get a notebook and some extra pencils just in case. A dictionary for challenging words may also be helpful.

Name _____ Date _____

**1.** There are many colorful sights that can be seen on a busy summer beach during the day. What are a few that stick out for you the most? Of those exciting sights, which one do you enjoy the most about the beach and why?

_____

_____

_____

_____

**2.** How do the sights of the summer beach change when the lights go down and nearly everybody goes home? Imagine that you're walking the beach on the night of a full moon. What do you see and how does it make you feel? Would you rather go to the beach during the day or the night and why?

_____

_____

_____

_____

          ©2012 Build Creative Writing Ideas

Name _____ Date _____

**3.** If you could go to see any landmark during summer vacation, what would it be and why? Describe how you think the landmark might look in great detail. Other than you, who would appreciate this destination the most and why?

_____

_____

_____

_____

_____

**4.** What is the ugliest summer vacation spot you and your family have ever gone to? What made it so unappealing? Why did you and your family go there in the first place?

_____

_____

_____

_____

_____

          ©2012 Build Creative Writing Ideas

Name _____ Date _____

**5.** Which of the following locations would you most want to see during
the summer and why: a baseball field, a theater stage, a mountaintop, or your own room? What
are some other places you'd like to see in the summer and why?

_____

_____

_____

_____

**6.** Which of the following locations would you least want to see during the summer and why: a
summer school classroom, the side of a highway for a community service trash pickup, your
locked room after getting grounded, or a polluted lake? How would you have ended up in that
location?

_____

_____

_____

_____

    **©2012 Build Creative Writing Ideas**

Name _____ Date _____

**7.** Describe a giant fireworks display in great detail including all of the different colors and shapes formed. Which would you say you enjoy more about fireworks, the sights or the sounds, and why? Would it be strange to watch fireworks without one or the other? Why or why not?

_____

_____

_____

_____

**8.** Some people want to see fireworks up close and try to set them off on their own. Why might that be a bad idea without an adult supervisor? What are some other dangerous things that people go to great lengths to see and why are they dangerous?

_____

_____

_____

_____

 ©2012 Build Creative Writing Ideas

Name _____ Date _____

**9.** Describe the beautiful sight of a table full of summer barbecue and side dishes. Explain why certain food items look good to you and why others might not.

_____

_____

_____

_____

**10.** Imagine that you've decided to throw a massive pool party and invite all of your friends. What are the decorations you would use to make sure that everything looks perfect? What would your guests think about the decor and the party in general?

_____

_____

_____

_____

          ©2012 Build Creative Writing Ideas

Name _____ Date _____

**11.** Describe the sound and feeling of a well-functioning air conditioner.
How do your summer activities revolve around places that have air conditioning? What would you do differently during the summer without air conditioning and why?

_____

_____

_____

_____

_____

**12.** What are some of the other cooling sounds of summer? How do you feel when you hear those sounds and why? Would you react differently if you heard the sounds during a colder season? Why or why not?

_____

_____

_____

_____

_____

     ©2012 Build Creative Writing Ideas

Name _____ Date _____

**13.** What are some examples of places that are quieter during the summer?
What are a few reasons for these locations to be less noisy? Do you think you'd enjoy visiting any
of these quieter places during the peaceful summer? Why or why not?

_____

_____

_____

_____

_____

**14.** What are a few places that are loud and crowded throughout the summer months? Which of
them do you enjoy the most and why? What is your favorite sound there and why?

_____

_____

_____

_____

    ©2012 Build Creative Writing Ideas

Name _____ Date _____

**15.** Imagine that you have woken up an hour before your fellow campers
at sleep-away camp. What are some sounds you might hear that they'd miss out on? Is having that
experience worth the loss of one hour of sleep? Why or why not?

_____

_____

_____

_____

**16.** How are the sounds of summer different in the country as opposed to the city? What are some
possible summer sounds in each? In which place would you rather spend your summer and why?

_____

_____

_____

_____

           ©2012 Build Creative Writing Ideas

Name _____ Date _____

**17.** The sun is blazing as you and your friends get ready for a wild summer obstacle course. What are some of the sounds all of you make as you run, sweat, and jump through the different obstacles? Would you earn the roar of the crowd at the end by winning? Why or why not?

_____

_____

_____

_____

**18.** How do people and things sound different when they're underwater at the pool or the beach? Describe trying to understand someone who is talking to you underwater. Are you able to figure him or her out? Why or why not?

_____

_____

_____

_____

©2012 Build Creative Writing Ideas

Name _____ Date _____

**19.** Summer is a time for travel, which means you'll be using plains,
trains, and automobiles. As you and your family head to summer vacation, what are some of the
sounds you might hear and why? How do you feel when you hear them and why?

_____

_____

_____

_____

_____

**20.** How do you think summer travel was different before trains, planes, and cars? What would
your family have used to get from place to place and how would that travel method sound? What
would some of the difficulties be in traveling that way and why?

_____

_____

_____

_____

                    ©2012 Build Creative Writing Ideas

Name _____ Date _____

**21.** As you try to convince your family to go to a nearby summer festival, a breeze blows the smells of the celebration your way. What are some of the distinct scents you can pick up? How might you use these aromas to get your family to go? Would the plan work? Why or why not?

_____

_____

_____

_____

**22.** The summer heat and wind can also cause some locations to smell very bad. What are a few examples of places you would not want to live next to in the summer and why? How would the worst offender of the bunch make you feel and why?

_____

_____

_____

_____

 ©2012 Build Creative Writing Ideas

Name _____ Date _____

**23.** How would you compare the smell of an ocean and beach with that of
a lake? Which scent do you find more appealing and why? Which location would be most fun to
spend a week at and why?

_____

_____

_____

_____

_____

**24.** How do each of the following wet summer smells makes you feel and why: a community
swimming pool, a freshly watered lawn, a car after a car wash, and a wet and furry dog?

_____

_____

_____

_____

_____

          ©2012 Build Creative Writing Ideas

Name _____ Date _____

**25.** Describe the barbecue grilling process from beginning to end using only your sense of smell. Which part of the process smells the best to you and why? Do you think grilling will be a big part of your life every summer? Why or why not?

_____

_____

_____

_____

_____

**26.** How does a big plate of grilled hamburgers and hot dogs smell to you? Do you think your feelings about the food would change if you were a vegetarian? What if you were allergic to hot dogs and hamburgers?

_____

_____

_____

_____

**©2012 Build Creative Writing Ideas**

Name _____ Date _____

**27.** It's very important to be protected from the sun all summer long by using sunscreen. Describe what your favorite sunscreen smells like to you. What does the scent of sunscreen remind you of and why?

_____

_____

_____

_____

_____

**28.** Imagine that you could create a sunscreen with any kind of aroma you wanted. What scent would you choose and why? Would it make you feel different about the object or type of food that the scent from your new sunscreen came from? Why or why not?

_____

_____

_____

_____

                                    **©2012 Build Creative Writing Ideas**

Name _____ Date _____

**29.** Summer is a season of sweat. What does the scent of being drenched
in sweat remind you of and why? Do you think it's OK to be sweaty during the hottest season of
the year? Why or why not?

_____

_____

_____

_____

_____

**30.** What is your most physical and active summer activity? How does it make you feel to be
moving around in the heat? What are some smells you associate with this activity and why?

_____

_____

_____

_____

_____

                                    ©2012 Build Creative Writing Ideas

Name _____ Date _____

**31.** You have bitten into a huge slice of watermelon. Describe how the juicy melon tastes and how the taste makes you feel. What are some events and places the taste of watermelon might make you think of and why?

_____

_____

_____

_____

_____

**32.** As part of a goofy contest, you must dig into a watermelon with your hands to try to find a clue inside. How does the pink melon feel against your fingers as you burrow through? How do you feel afterwards when you're covered in seeds, melon and juice? Do you like the feeling? Why or why not?

_____

_____

_____

_____

 **©2012 Build Creative Writing Ideas**

Name _____ Date _____

**33.** Quite accidentally, you've swallowed some pool or ocean water while playing with your friends. How would you describe the taste? What would you most want to eat afterward to try to get the taste out of your mouth and why?

_____

_____

_____

_____

_____

**34.** After taking a dip in the water and rolling around on the beach, you are completely covered in sand. How does the sand feel on your skin? Where does it feel the strangest and why? What will you do to rid yourself of this sandy outer layer?

_____

_____

_____

_____

_____

     ©2012 Build Creative Writing Ideas

Name _____ Date _____

**35.** How would you describe the taste of your favorite summer food? In what situation would you usually eat this seasonal delicacy and why? How do you think a famous chef would make it differently from the way it's normally made for you and why?

_____

_____

_____

_____

_____

**36.** Imagine that you were the chef putting this meal together. In what ways would you have to get your hands dirty to cook it? How would touching the food feel? What would your cooking difficulties be and why?

_____

_____

_____

_____

            ©2012 Build Creative Writing Ideas

Name _____ Date _____

**37.** Summer wouldn't be summer without an ice cream treat to keep the temperature at bay. What flavors and toppings would you include in your ideal ice cream creation? How would all of them taste together? Is there anything that could make your dessert even better? Why or why not?

_____

_____

_____

_____

_____

**38.** After finishing your ice cream, you realize that it's all over your face and hands. How does the sugary sweet treat feel as it sticks to your skin? What would you do to clean it off? How do you feel differently when it's all cleaned off and why?

_____

_____

_____

_____

 **©2012 Build Creative Writing Ideas**

Name _____ Date _____

**39.** While they're not meant to be eaten, sometimes we accidentally get a taste of sunscreen or bug spray during the summer. How does the taste of these chemicals make you feel? What is it important to avoid getting too much of these products in your mouth?

_____

_____

_____

_____

**40.** When you completely avoid sunscreen and bug spray, you end up with a summer sunburn and bug bites. How would you describe the feeling of a sunburn? How would you describe how a bug bite feels? Which would you say is the most irritating and why?

_____

_____

_____

_____

 ©2012 Build Creative Writing Ideas

Name _____ Date _____

**41.** Summer has a way of bringing the community together. What are some activities during the summer that tend to have a lot of people involved? What is it like seeing all these different people together in the same place?

_____

_____

_____

_____

_____

**42.** The community must also come together during negative summer occurrences like a drought or a wildfire. What are some ways that people need to function together during a summer crisis? How might you and your family contribute during such an event and why?

_____

_____

_____

_____

 ©2012 Build Creative Writing Ideas

Name _____ Date _____

**43.** Summer can be a time for big group trips with a camp or youth group.
What is a place you'd enjoy visiting during the summer with a bunch of people? What would you enjoy about having so many people there with you and why?

_____

_____

_____

_____

**44.** What are some summer destinations that you'd rather go to with a smaller group? Who would you pick to be in this intimate group and why? What are the benefits of having fewer people around and why?

_____

_____

_____

_____

 ©2012 Build Creative Writing Ideas

Name _____ Date _____

**45.** Imagine that you were an athlete training all summer to be ready for a fall sport like football, soccer or cross country. Would you try to get any friends or other people you know to help? Why or why not? What would be the most difficult part of the training and why?

_____

_____

_____

_____

**46.** Aside from athletic achievement, what other goals might you set for yourself in the three months off from school and why? Do you think it's important to know where you're headed or that its better to go with the flow? Why?

_____

_____

_____

_____

    ©2012 Build Creative Writing Ideas

Name _____ Date _____

**47.** Imagine that you have joined a garage band with your friends and that
you practice every day during the summer. What is your role in the band and what kind of music
do you play? How will things change when summer comes to an end and why?

_____

_____

_____

_____

**48.** Your band has become a huge success and you are going to spend all next summer touring
around the country. What would you enjoy the most about seeing all these new cities during the
summer and why? What would you miss about your hometown during the summer and why?

_____

_____

_____

_____

             ©2012 Build Creative Writing Ideas

Name _____ Date _____

**49.** The members of your school board have approved a resolution that will require all students to go to school all summer long. What would you think about all-year schooling? What are some things you and your family would miss out on if you didn't have three straight months off?

_____

_____

_____

_____

**50.** You have decided to fight back against the all-year school resolution. Who would you recruit for your team to save the summer and why? What would your team do to try to get the rule repealed and why?

_____

_____

_____

_____

   ©2012 Build Creative Writing Ideas

Name _____ Date _____

**51.** What is your first thought when you see a bunch of fall leaves gathered in your backyard? Is it a positive or a negative thought and why? Would the other members of your family feel the same way? Why or why not?

_____

_____

_____

_____

**52.** How might a bird or a squirrel feel upon seeing the leaves fall to the ground and why? What might their first action be to prepare for the changing of the seasons and why?

_____

_____

_____

_____

          ©2012 Build Creative Writing Ideas

Name _____ Date _____

**53.** How would you react if you saw an actual ghost on Halloween?
Would you say anything to the ghost and, if so, what and why? Would other people be able to see
the ghost, too? Why or why not?

_____

_____

_____

_____

**54.** Do you believe in ghosts? Why or why not? Have you seen anything in your life that might
lead you to believe in things we can't explain? Why or why not?

_____

_____

_____

_____

          ©2012 Build Creative Writing Ideas

Name _____ Date _____

**55.** What is the most interesting pumpkin you've ever seen in your life?
What was it that made it so unique: the shape, the size, the color or something else entirely? What do you think happened to that pumpkin and why?

_____

_____

_____

_____

_____

**56.** Whether it be because of pumpkin assault or decay, pumpkins don't last forever. How does it make you feel when you see a smashed or rotten pumpkin and why? How might the pumpkin feel itself and why?

_____

_____

_____

_____

                                    **©2012 Build Creative Writing Ideas**

Name _____ Date _____

**57.** What are some of the sights of fall that make you truly feel that fall has arrived? Are you glad when you see them? Why or why not? What does the arrival of fall mean to you?

_____

_____

_____

_____

**58.** What are some sights you might see that clue you into the end of fall? How does seeing the end of fall before your eyes make you feel and why? What does the departure of fall mean to you and why?

_____

_____

_____

_____

          ©2012 Build Creative Writing Ideas

Name _____ Date _____

**59.** If you could choose any place in the world that you'd have to see at least once every fall for the rest of your life, where would it be and why? What sorts of things would you do there and how would those things change as you get older?

_____

_____

_____

_____

**60.** Artistic people tend to see fall as a time of sadness, but how do you see it? Do you think fall should be connected with any type of emotion? Why or why not?

_____

_____

_____

_____

©2012 Build Creative Writing Ideas

Name _____ Date _____

**61.** Describe the sound of your feet coming crashing down on a pile of leaves. What does that series of crinkles and crunches make you think of and why? Does it remind you of any sounds that other things make? Why or why not?

_____

_____

_____

_____

**62.** If a leaf could make a sound like an animal, what sound would it make and why? What would some other fall plants and vegetables sound like? How would fall be different with barking leaves and hissing pumpkins and why?

_____

_____

_____

_____

 **©2012 Build Creative Writing Ideas**

Name _____ Date _____

**63.** If you could pick a song to listen to during the fall, what would it be
and why? In what ways does the song make you think of the season and why? Would your family
members agree with you? Why or why not?

_____

_____

_____

_____

**64.** Which musical instruments or styles of music make you think of fall the most and why?
Describe what a fall concert of only these instruments and styles might be like. Would you enjoy
it? Why or why not?

_____

_____

_____

_____

©2012 Build Creative Writing Ideas

Name _____ Date _____

**65.** What are some spooky fall sounds that you might associate with Halloween? How do those sounds make you feel and why? Which one would scare you the most and why?

_____

_____

_____

_____

_____

**66.** What is it about being in the dark that makes noises, especially creepy Halloween noises, even scarier? What noise do you think would scare you the most if you were sitting in a pitch-black room and why?

_____

_____

_____

_____

 ©2012 Build Creative Writing Ideas

Name _____ Date _____

**67.** The sights, smells, and tastes of Thanksgiving are so prevalent, it's hard to remember the sounds. What are some of the sounds that occur around your holiday table? Which sound do you enjoy the most, which do you enjoy the least, and why?

_____

_____

_____

_____

**68.** What sounds do your family members make while actually eating the Thanksgiving meal? Would you say your family members have good table manners? Why or why not? Are your table manners near the top, near the bottom or somewhere in the middle compared to the rest of your family and why?

_____

_____

_____

_____

 ©2012 Build Creative Writing Ideas

Name _____ Date _____

**69.** What are some of the sounds that the animals of fall make? How might these sounds be related to their survival? Do any of their sounds scare you? Why or why not?

_____

_____

_____

_____

_____

**70.** What are a few sounds that humans make during the fall? Are these sounds related to fun or survival and why? Which of these sounds would you consider to be the most important for people and why?

_____

_____

_____

_____

_____

 ©2012 Build Creative Writing Ideas

Name _____ Date _____

**71.** Describe the smell of a freshly baked pumpkin pie right out of the oven. How does the aroma make you feel, knowing that in a few short minutes you'll be able to eat it? How would your feeling change if there were many different kinds of pies fresh out of the oven and why?

_____

_____

_____

_____

**72.** Would you feel any differently if you were a bird perched on the windowsill hoping to get a nibble of that tasty-smelling pie? What would you and your bird friends do to try to get your wings on that dessert? Would you be successful? Why or why not?

_____

_____

_____

_____

                                    **©2012 Build Creative Writing Ideas**

Name _____ Date _____

**73.** The fall is a season of pungent spices. What are some of your favorite herb and spice smells during the fall and why? What spice-related memories might smelling the spices conjure up and why?

_____

_____

_____

_____

**74.** Even with spices, there can be too much of a good thing. How might you feel if you accidentally inhaled way too much cinnamon, cloves, or another spice? What other smells in your life have you taken in too much of and what did you do to correct the problem?

_____

_____

_____

_____

 ©2012 Build Creative Writing Ideas

Name _____ Date _____

**75.** Would you say the fall air in your town smells differently than it does during the other seasons? If so, how would you describe the difference? Aside from being a different temperature, how does the season *feel* different and why?

_____

_____

_____

_____

**76.** What are some of the grossest, most pungent odors you can think of connected with the fall? Which one is the most disgusting and why? What would you do if your room intensely smelled like that odor for some reason?

_____

_____

_____

_____

                                                  ©2012 Build Creative Writing Ideas

Name _____ Date _____

**77.** Describe all the smells you can remember from your most recent Thanksgiving dinner. Which one sticks out the most and why? If you could smell any scent from that dinner frequently throughout the year, which one would it be and why?

_____

_____

_____

_____

_____

**78.** What is a smell that you think could ruin your Thanksgiving dinner? What would your family do to find a way around it and why? Which of your family members would be the most likely to complain about it?

_____

_____

_____

_____

 ©2012 Build Creative Writing Ideas

Name _____ Date _____

**79.** What is the first smell you can ever remember from the fall season?
Why do you think it's stuck with you for all these years? What other things happened in connection with that smell and how does the smell make you feel?

_____

_____

_____

_____

**80.** What is the most recent fall smell that really connected with you? Was it a positive or a negative smell and why? Do you think the scent would have connected with someone else too? Why or why not?

_____

_____

_____

_____

     ©2012 Build Creative Writing Ideas

Name _____ Date _____

**81.** How does the taste of the first Halloween candy of the night taste differently from the last candy of the night? Why might the two taste different from each other even if they're the same type of candy? How much candy would you say is too much candy and why?

_____

_____

_____

_____

_____

**82.** Eating some Halloween candies is a very tactile experience. Describe unwrapping several different kinds of candy and what goes into actually getting to the tasty treat itself. Which kind of candy do you most enjoy tearing into and why: a foil wrapper, a plastic wrapper, a paper wrapper, a paper package to tear into, or something else entirely?

_____

_____

_____

_____

                                          **©2012 Build Creative Writing Ideas**

Name _____ Date _____

**83.** Of all the Thanksgiving meals you've eaten, would you say one ranks the highest as far as taste is concerned? Why or why not? Of the cooks in your Thanksgiving kitchen, who is the best cook and why? What tips might you take from him or her to become a good cook on your own someday and why?

_____

_____

_____

_____

**84.** Imagine you had multiple Thanksgiving dishes lined up next to each other just to feel what it was like to touch them. The dishes include gravy, stuffing, Jell-O, and at least two others. Describe what each of them feels like on your hands. Which one might be the strangest sensation and why?

_____

_____

_____

_____

 ©2012 Build Creative Writing Ideas

Name _____ Date _____

**85.** Describe the taste of a warm, spiced apple cider. Try to identify the different parts of the taste, such as what might be coming from the apples and what might be from other sources. How do you think the people who create the cider figure out their own blend of apples and spices?

_____

_____

_____

_____

**86.** To make a little extra money, you are helping out at the local apple orchard as a picker. How would you describe how the different kinds of apples feel as you pull them down? Is there a difference between picking apples for fun and picking apples as a job? Why or why not?

_____

_____

_____

_____

          **©2012 Build Creative Writing Ideas**

Name _____ Date _____

**87.** What are some of the food staples for breakfast, lunch, and dinner in your house during the fall? Are there any that you look forward to the rest of the year? Why or why not? Describe which meal tastes the best and why. How is that taste distinct from other foods and why?

_____

_____

_____

_____

**88.** Describe the difference your hands would feel from crumpling up a handful of wet leaves versus crumpling up a handful of dry leaves. What happens to the leaves and why? How do your hands feel after crushing both? Which would you rather dive into and why: a pile of wet leaves or a pile of dry leaves?

_____

_____

_____

_____

          ©2012 Build Creative Writing Ideas

Name _____ Date _____

**89.** If you were a squirrel, you'd have a completely different diet from the one you have as a human. You'd eat nuts if you could find them and rummage through the trash if you couldn't. How do you think a squirrel's sense of taste differs from yours? In what ways are you more picky than a squirrel when it comes to what you'll eat and why?

_____

_____

_____

_____

**90.** Squirrels have the amazing ability to climb up trees and jump from branch to branch. If you were a squirrel, how do you think it would feel to grip the branches as you ran and leapt? What would your parents say if they saw you trying to run up a tree like a squirrel?

_____

_____

_____

_____

  ©2012 Build Creative Writing Ideas

Name _____ Date _____

**91.** How would you describe fall in your town? Is it a time for people to come together, a season in which people tend to keep to themselves, or something else entirely? How do you think your town has changed for the fall season in the last 50 years and why?

_____

_____

_____

_____

_____

**92.** What would you say makes your town unique during the fall and why? How is your town similar to other areas in the fall and why? Which would you say is your town's most unique season and why?

_____

_____

_____

_____

_____

     ©2012 Build Creative Writing Ideas

Name _____ Date _____

**93.** Imagine that you are going trick-or-treating with a large group of families and friends. Who are the most likely people to be in that group and why? What would you differently with that group than you would if it was just you and your parents and why?

_____

_____

_____

_____

**94.** What costumes might your group members wear and why? Describe what outfits these friends and family members might wear based on their preferences and personalities.

_____

_____

_____

_____

 ©2012 Build Creative Writing Ideas

Name _____ Date _____

**95.** You and your friends have been turned into a pile of leaves! What will you do to get out of this situation before you all get raked?

_____

_____

_____

_____

_____

**96.** How do you think trees feel when they lose their leaves? Imagine that a bare tree began talking to you about the season. What would it say and why?

_____

_____

_____

_____

_____

       ©2012 Build Creative Writing Ideas

Name _____ Date _____

**97.** If you could cast a bunch of famous actors and celebrities to play your family members for one Thanksgiving, who would they be and why? How would the holiday be different with people *playing* your family as opposed to actually being your family? Why?

_____

_____

_____

_____

**98.** If your family was replaced by actors for one year's Thanksgiving, what would you miss the most about them and why? Why is it important to be with your *actual* family for turkey day?

_____

_____

_____

_____

 **©2012 Build Creative Writing Ideas**

Name _____ Date _____

**99.** Imagine that you had no phone or games to play while you were
sitting outside in a forest full of red, purple, and yellow leaves. Are you more likely to appreciate
the beauty of the season or be bored? Why? How does fall nature make you feel and why?

_____

_____

_____

_____

**100.** Which of your family members other than you is most likely to appreciate fall nature and
why? What is it about this person that makes him or her enjoy fall's foliage more? What are some
things nature has that technology doesn't?

_____

_____

_____

_____

 ©2012 Build Creative Writing Ideas

Name _____ Date _____

**101.** How does it feel to wake up and see the world covered by a blanket of white snow? What is the first thing you would do and why? Would your feeling change if you found out you still had school? Why or why not?

_____

_____

_____

_____

**102.** Imagine that the snow was piled so high that it completely blocked your window. Would your feeling be any different? How would your parents feel if they saw the snow piled that high and why?

_____

_____

_____

_____

 **©2012 Build Creative Writing Ideas**

Name _____ Date _____

**103.** What would you do if you saw a person slip on an icy patch of sidewalk and why? Would you do the same thing if it was a family member or a complete stranger and why?

_____

_____

_____

_____

**104.** How would your reaction change if you saw a car spin out and crash into a snow embankment? Do you think that most people would do the same thing as you? Why or why not?

_____

_____

_____

_____

 ©2012 Build Creative Writing Ideas

Name _____ Date _____

**105.** What is the most memorable thing you've ever seen during the winter and why? What would have made the event less memorable? How would your memory change if you heard about it in a story instead of experiencing it first hand?

_____

_____

_____

_____

**106.** How do you think the event would have been different if you were blind and could only use your other sense to observe it? Would it have been as memorable? Why or why not?

_____

_____

_____

_____

 **©2012 Build Creative Writing Ideas**

Name _____ Date _____

**107.** How do you feel when you see a large pile of Christmas, Hanukkah, or Kwanzaa gifts and why? Do you ever do anything special to try to figure out what the gifts are? Why or why not?

_____

_____

_____

_____

**108.** How would the sight of all those gifts affect you differently if you were very poor? Why is it important to remember people who are less fortunate than you during the holiday season?

_____

_____

_____

_____

 ©2012 Build Creative Writing Ideas

Name _____ Date _____

**109.** Which of the following events would you rather see and why: the Winter Olympics, the Super Bowl, New Year's Eve in Times Square, New York, the lighting of the biggest Christmas tree in the world?

_____

_____

_____

_____

**110.** How would attending that event make you feel and why? Who would you want to accompany you and why? How would the event be different if you saw it alone?

_____

_____

_____

_____

                                        **©2012 Build Creative Writing Ideas**

Name _____ Date _____

**111.** What does the sound of a massive, diesel-powered snow plow going by your house make you think of and why? Would it make your parents think of something different than you? Why or why not?

_____

_____

_____

_____

**112.** How might you feel about the sound if you were the one driving the plow? Would you take pride in your job? What would you enjoy the most about your job plowing the streets and why?

_____

_____

_____

_____

 ©2012 Build Creative Writing Ideas

Name _____ Date _____

**113.** As you look out into the vast snowy landscape, you hear a gust of wind blowing the snow from one hill to another. If the winter wind could talk, what would it say and why? How would you respond to the howls of wind and why?

_____

_____

_____

_____

**114.** Create a poem or a song that describes how the winter wind sounds differently than the wind of other seasons. Include how the different seasonal winds make you feel and why for a personal touch.

_____

_____

_____

_____

 **©2012 Build Creative Writing Ideas**

Name _____ Date _____

**115.** When the roads are covered in snow, the sound that can stand out the most is the sound of silence. How does the quiet and white road make you feel in comparison to its usual noise level and why? Is there anything you are more or less likely to do because of the quiet and why?

_____

_____

_____

_____

**116.** If you lived in a frequently snow-covered area, would you get sick of the quiet? Why or why not? What sounds would you most want to hear if you hadn't heard any in a while and why?

_____

_____

_____

_____

          ©2012 Build Creative Writing Ideas

Name _____ Date _____

**117.** It seems like the entire neighborhood is gathered at the top of the steepest hill in town. Describe the sounds of all the kids as they sled, tube, and dive down the snow-packed hill. Which of the sounds do you like, which do you dislike, and why?

_____

_____

_____

_____

**118.** How do you think the way sounds of kids sledding and enjoying themselves make you feel will change as you get older? Will you be jealous, annoyed or something completely different and why? Would this feeling change if it was your own kids playing? Why or why not?

_____

_____

_____

_____

 **©2012 Build Creative Writing Ideas**

Name _____ Date _____

**119.** What are some of the sounds you hear around your home in the
winter that you wouldn't normally hear in other seasons? How do those sounds make you feel and
what sounds might you use to respond to them?

_____

_____

_____

_____

**120.** You hear a large group of Christmas carolers down the street heading toward your house.
How will you and your family react and why? Would you react differently if you were a different
religion or lived in a different neighborhood?

_____

_____

_____

_____

 **©2012 Build Creative Writing Ideas**

Name _____ Date _____

**121.** The holiday season can be a bit overwhelming with the delicious
smells of Christmas, Hanukkah, and other festivities. Which is your favorite of the holiday smells
and why? What would that smell make you think of it you happened to get a whiff of it while
walking down the street and why?

_____

_____

_____

_____

**122.** Gathering with family during the season can bring a great many odors together, from your
aunt's perfume to the baby powder of a newborn cousin. What is your most memorable family
smell from your most recent winter holiday gathering and why? Is it memorable in a good way or
a bad way and why?

_____

_____

_____

_____

 **©2012 Build Creative Writing Ideas**

Name _____ Date _____

**123.** After a long weekend day of playing in the snow, what scent would
you most want to smell upon returning home and why? What does that smell usually mean is
about to happen and why?

_____

_____

_____

_____

**124.** After that day of play, what would you least want to smell and why? How would that smell
make you feel and why? What would you do to avoid that smell and its consequences and why?

_____

_____

_____

_____

     ©2012 Build Creative Writing Ideas

Name _____ Date _____

**125.** How would you describe the smell of a winter's day? If you were to take in that smell during a different season, what would it make you think of and how would it make you feel? Do you like the smell? Why or why not?

_____

_____

_____

_____

**126.** How does winter smell differently compared to the other three seasons? How would it make you feel if you noticed the aroma of winter more than a month early and why? Would the possibility of extra winter excite you or disappoint you and why?

_____

_____

_____

_____

                                    ©2012 Build Creative Writing Ideas

Name _____ Date _____

**127.** As you take off your many winter layers, you notice that even you smell a little different during the season. How has your scent changed in the wintertime and is it for better or worse? Would that aroma alteration cause you to make any changes? Why or why not?

_____

_____

_____

_____

**128.** If you could choose a smell of winter to bottle up and wear as a cologne or perfume, what would it be and why? How would people react differently to you if you smelled like that aspect of winter and why?

_____

_____

_____

_____

          **©2012 Build Creative Writing Ideas**

Name _____ Date _____

**129.** How do you think the smell of winter has changed in the last century with more cars on the road, ice-melting chemical salt, and snow blowers? How would your neighborhood smell differently way back then and why? In what other ways would your area be different?

_____

_____

_____

_____

**130.** How might the smells of winter change in the next 100 years and why? Would new technology produce better-smelling chemicals or worse-smelling ones? Will the winter become more or less environmentally friendly and why?

_____

_____

_____

_____

 **©2012 Build Creative Writing Ideas**

Name _____ Date _____

**131.** How would you describe the taste of snow? Why do you think people enjoy sticking their tongues out during a snowfall? If you could give any flavor to snow, what would it be and why?

_____

_____

_____

_____

**132.** You are holding a huge snowball in your glove-protected hand. How does the texture of the snow feel through the glove? How would it feel differently if you weren't wearing gloves and why?

_____

_____

_____

_____

**©2012 Build Creative Writing Ideas**

Name _____ Date _____

**133.** There are many different varieties of hot chocolate you could drink during the winter, including from a packet, with or without marshmallows, and topped with whipped cream. What do you think is the best-tasting hot chocolate in the world and why? Describe the taste of this treat in great detail.

_____

_____

_____

_____

**134.** Imagine that your hands are absolutely freezing until someone gives you a cup of hot cocoa to hold onto. How does the toasty cup feel on your hands? Why is it important to keep your hands warm during the winter?

_____

_____

_____

_____

 **©2012 Build Creative Writing Ideas**

Name _____ Date _____

**135.** What is your favorite taste of the holiday season and why? Would this be a taste you'd want to have all year long? Why or why not? Would it still be as special if you had it every day? Why or why not?

_____

_____

_____

_____

**136.** Imagine that you have just picked up your first gift to open during the holidays. How do the wrapping paper and tape feel against your hands? How do you feel when you finally get to tear into it and find out what it is and why?

_____

_____

_____

_____

 **©2012 Build Creative Writing Ideas**

Name _____ Date _____

**137.** Your family has decided to sit by the fireplace and have your favorite winter dish. Describe all of the courses of the meal and how they taste. Does the meal change at all because you're eating it by the toasty fire? Why or why not?

_____

_____

_____

_____

**138.** How does the warmth from the fireplace feel on your skin? How does it change the way you feel on a cold winter's night? How might a winter indoor fireplace feel different than an outdoor campfire during the spring or fall?

_____

_____

_____

_____

Name _____ Date _____

**139.** Is there anything your parents drink or eat during the winter that you dislike? If so, what is it and what does it taste like to you? If not, come up with a made-up food or drink and describe why you dislike it.

_____

_____

_____

_____

**140.** There are many winter items like matches, kerosene and lighters that kids aren't allowed to touch. Why do you think it's a good idea for children not to touch these fire-starting objects and substances? What are some other winter items you aren't allowed to touch in your house and why can't you touch them?

_____

_____

_____

_____

                    ©2012 Build Creative Writing Ideas

Name _____ Date _____

**141.** How do you think the country would be different if we were in the middle of a wintry ice age? What are some ways that you and your family would do things differently and why?

_____

_____

_____

_____

**142.** If there were an ice age afoot, how would the country's economy change? How would it effect agriculture, shipping, and air travel? How do you think we as a nation would adapt to the weather and why?

_____

_____

_____

_____

Name _____ Date _____

**143.** What are some ways in which a town can come together to fight back against a winter storm? Who are some of the people who need to communicate during a storm and why? What is the end result of these people working together?

_____

_____

_____

_____

**144.** What would happen if these people failed to work together during some harsh winter weather? What problems might your town face and why? What would you do to try to improve the situation and why?

_____

_____

_____

_____

 ©2012 Build Creative Writing Ideas

Name _____ Date _____

**145.** You have been tasked with thawing out and starting a car that has been completely frozen over with a thick sheet of ice. What would you do to get it loose? Who would you ask to help and why? Would you be successful? Why or why not?

_____

_____

_____

_____

**146.** How might your tactics change if you were a rescue worker and there was a very cold person trapped inside the icy vehicle? Describe how you'd get the person out of the car and what you'd do afterward to make sure he or she was alright.

_____

_____

_____

_____

Name _____ Date _____

**147.** If you lived in a consistently cold and icy climate, do you think you'd
be drawn to an ice-related sport like ice hockey or figure skating? Why or why not? Would there
be any sports you play now that you wouldn't be able to participate in? Why or why not?

_____

_____

_____

_____

**148.** Imagine that you are the goaltender in an outdoor ice hockey game with over 100,000 people
watching you. How do you feel and why? What are some ways that you handle the pressure? Do
you think you would win? Why or why not?

_____

_____

_____

_____

**©2012 Build Creative Writing Ideas**

Name _____ Date _____

**149.** Who is someone you know who strongly dislikes the winter? What does he or she have such an issue with the season? If you wanted to convince this person that winter was awesome, what would you do and why?

_____

_____

_____

_____

**150.** People living in certain climates have never experienced a cold, snowy, and icy winter. How might they be unprepared for the season if they took a vacation to a wintry place and why? How would you personally help this person and why?

_____

_____

_____

_____

 ©2012 Build Creative Writing Ideas

Name _____ Date _____

**151.** Watching a flower bloom during the spring is not a one-hour event that you could take in during one sitting. There are many tiny steps along the way until the flower has completely bloomed. Would you have the patience to check back with a blooming flower every day to view each step? Why or why not? What are some other ways that nature requires patience?

_____

_____

_____

_____

**152.** What would you classify as the most exciting process to watch unfold in nature during the spring and why? Why do you think most people would rather look at a computer screen or phone instead of nature? If you had a choice between the two, which would you rather watch and why?

_____

_____

_____

_____

 ©2012 Build Creative Writing Ideas

Name _____ Date _____

**153.** There are many beautiful gardens and landscapes throughout the world. If you were to guess which of these places was the most breathtaking, which country or city would you guess and why? Would you rather go there with your family or alone to take in the sight and why?

_____

_____

_____

_____

**154.** If you lived in this beautiful place and saw the same amazing sights every single day, do you think it would change your attitude about the importance of nature? Why or why not? What are some ways that your life would be different living in such a picturesque place and why?

_____

_____

_____

_____

 **©2012 Build Creative Writing Ideas**

Name _____ Date _____

**155.** What is your typical reaction when you see a big plate full of spring vegetables in front of you at the dinner table and why? Does the fact that the vegetables are healthy for you make a difference? Why or why not? How much do you usually finish?

_____

_____

_____

_____

_____

**156.** Imagine that it's 20 or more years in the future and you have kids and a garden full of fresh spring vegetables. Would you try to force your children to eat the veggies even if they didn't want them? If so, how would you try to make them appreciate the sight of vegetables? If not, what would you feed them instead and why?

_____

_____

_____

_____

                                         ©2012 Build Creative Writing Ideas

Name _____ Date _____

**157.** How do your parents deal with the spring sight of grass that has grown too high around your house? Do they cut the grass themselves? If not, do they hire someone or just let it grow as tall as it can? Do you think that freshly cut grass looks better than an overgrown lawn? Why or why not?

_____

_____

_____

_____

**158.** How might someone cutting the grass look to you if you were an ant living in the ground? Would it be frightening or cool, and why? What other aspects of spring would look different from the perspective of an ant and how would they make you feel?

_____

_____

_____

_____

     **©2012 Build Creative Writing Ideas**

Name _____ Date _____

**159.** Your parents have come home with tickets to a spring sporting event.
Which kind of spring sport would you be the most excited to see and why? Which type of event would you be least excited to see? How would you best try to enjoy the event you aren't that interested in?

_____

_____

_____

_____

_____

**160.** Seeing a spring event like a spring training baseball game can be amazing as a kid, but do you think it's just as amazing for the players? If you were a player, what would the sight of a baseball field make you think of, considering that it's your job? Do you think it would be difficult to stay excited? Why or why not?

_____

_____

_____

_____

 **©2012 Build Creative Writing Ideas**

Name _____ Date _____

**161.** The springtime morning can be filled with the sounds of birds chirping away. How does hearing a bunch of birds singing make you feel and why? Would you feel differently if they were singing on a weekend or a vacation and why?

_____

_____

_____

_____

_____

**162.** If you could understand bird language, what do you think the bird songs would mean? What would you talk to the birds about if you could speak bird as well? How would the birds react to a human singing bird songs and why?

_____

_____

_____

_____

_____

            ©2012 Build Creative Writing Ideas

Name _____ Date _____

**163.** Often thought of as an unanswerable spring question, if a tree falls in the woods and nobody is around to hear it, does it make a sound? Why or why not?

_____

_____

_____

_____

**164.** What are some other questionable sounds that could occur in a forest without anybody knowing about them? What would it be like to live alone in the middle of the woods and be the only person to hear these sounds? Why?

_____

_____

_____

_____

 ©2012 Build Creative Writing Ideas

Name _____ Date _____

**165.** Since spring is a season that can cause allergies, a frequent spring sound is the sound of a sneeze. What is your typical first reaction when you hear a sneeze and why? Do you say or do anything when you hear a sneeze? Why or why not?

_____

_____

_____

_____

**166.** Many different people have very unique sneezes. Which one of your friends has the loudest and most boisterous sneeze? Would you say that sneeze fits with his or her personality? Why or why not? How would you describe your own sneeze?

_____

_____

_____

_____

                                      ©2012 Build Creative Writing Ideas

Name _____ Date _____

**167.** Some sounds during the spring can be frightening, like the buzzing of
a bee or a hive of bees. What are the scariest sounds you can think of that you might hear in
nature? How would you react if you heard those sounds and why?

_____

_____

_____

_____

**168.** While we may be afraid of some insects and animals, often they're the ones who are afraid of
us. What are some sounds that humans make that might scare a forest creature? What are some
machine sounds that could frighten animals? How might you react to the sounds if you were an
animal and why?

_____

_____

_____

_____

 ©2012 Build Creative Writing Ideas

Name _____ Date _____

**169.** If you were designing a spring video game, what sounds of the
season would you include and why? How realistic do you think you'd be able to make the sounds
from the game and why? What would the game be about and why?

_____

_____

_____

_____

_____

**170.** Who that you know would rather hear the sounds of spring from a video game as opposed to
experiencing them in nature and why? Why do you think it's important to go out and experience
nature during the spring? What are some of the benefits of the fresh air and the activity?

_____

_____

_____

_____

          ©2012 Build Creative Writing Ideas

Name _____ Date _____

**171.** What are some smells that remind you the most of spring? What are some spring memories you might think of while smelling those scents? How would you react the first time you smelled them during the season and why?

_____

_____

_____

_____

**172.** How do you think the following places would smell differently during the spring and why: New York City, a cow pasture, a lakeside property, and the tropical rainforest?

_____

_____

_____

_____

 **©2012 Build Creative Writing Ideas**

Name _____ Date _____

**173.** How would you describe the smell of a fresh herb garden? Which of
the herbs would stand out the most to you and why? Are there any herbs you wouldn't eat in a
million years? Why or why not?

_____

_____

_____

_____

**174.** How would you react to the smell of a fresh herb garden if you were a bunny? What would
you do to try to sneak into the garden to have some lunch? Would you get caught? Why or why
not?

_____

_____

_____

_____

Name _____ Date _____

**175.** Of all the flowers you've ever smelled, which one had the most
appealing scent and why? How hard do you think it would be to plant a garden full of those
flowers and why? Who would you get to help you and why?

_____

_____

_____

_____

**176.** How do you think flowers smell to a bee? Describe what might be going through the mind of
a bee as she excitedly dances from flower to flower. Is there anything in your life you get as
enthusiastic about? Why or why not?

_____

_____

_____

_____

          ©2012 Build Creative Writing Ideas

Name _____ Date _____

**177.** As the saying goes, it's important to stop and smell the roses. What do you think this saying means? Would you agree with it? Why or why not?

_____

_____

_____

_____

**178.** What are some ways that you can "stop and smell the roses" during the spring both literally and figuratively? What usually goes through your mind when you get a chance to relax and take in your surroundings? How often do you think a person should practice this habit and why?

_____

_____

_____

_____

 **©2012 Build Creative Writing Ideas**

Name _____ Date _____

**179.** What are some smells of spring that completely turn you off and
why? What would you do if your parents bought an air freshener that smelled exactly like the
worst of those smells? How would it make you feel and why?

_____

_____

_____

_____

**180.** Based on your enjoyment of spring aromas, would you consider yourself a spring person?
Why or why not? Out of all the people you know, who would you say is the springiest person and
why? Which season do you connect with the most and why?

_____

_____

_____

_____

 ©2012 Build Creative Writing Ideas

Name _____ Date _____

**181.** You are biting into a fresh spring salad of raw vegetables. Would you enjoy the taste of the salad without any kind of dressing? Why or why not? Which of the vegetables would stick out flavor-wise the most and why?

_____

_____

_____

_____

**182.** If you were a gardener, which vegetable do you think you'd enjoy harvesting the most and why? Do you think you would gain a different connection with the food by handling it before it reached your table? Why or why not?

_____

_____

_____

_____

 ©2012 Build Creative Writing Ideas

Name _____ Date _____

**183.** Do you think food tastes differently when you eat it outside during a spring picnic? Why or why not? What are some of the tastiest foods you'd bring along on your picnic and why?

_____

_____

_____

_____

**184.** Some people feel a need to sit on the ground every once in a while and run their hands through the grass to feel connected with the earth. How do you think they feel when they have the opportunity to do so? Do you feel similarly when you're out in nature? Why or why not?

_____

_____

_____

_____

 ©2012 Build Creative Writing Ideas

Name _____ Date _____

**185.** Imagine that you were looking forward to biting into a juicy, red apple but it tasted extremely strange. Upon looking at your hand, you realize you were actually eating a tomato. How does the tomato taste differently from how the apple would have tasted? How do you feel about the mistake you made and why?

_____

_____

_____

_____

**186.** After doing your terrible stand-up comedy routine on stage, the audience has pelted you with dozens of tomatoes. Describe the feeling of the tomato pulp running down your skin. What is an example of a bad joke the audience didn't like?

_____

_____

_____

_____

 ©2012 Build Creative Writing Ideas

Name _____ Date _____

**187.** Describe a spring meal you look forward to every year. Explain how each food tastes to you and why you enjoy it so much. What ingredients do you think are the most important to make it taste exactly how you like it and why?

_____

_____

_____

_____

_____

**188.** Imagine that you were a cook getting ready to prepare a spring meal. Would you rather handle ingredients that were fresh, frozen, or canned and why? Which do you think would result in the best-tasting meal and why?

_____

_____

_____

_____

                                    ©2012 Build Creative Writing Ideas

Name _____ Date _____

**189.** Think ahead to the future when you're a mother or a father. What would your ideal breakfast in bed be and why? Describe how each ingredient would taste. Would the meal taste differently because your children made it? Why or why not?

_____

_____

_____

_____

_____

**190.** You and your family members are stitching together a green spring quilt to give as a gift to your relatives. Describe how you might need to use your sense of touch in putting the quilt together. How would the quilt feel if you took a nap underneath it and why?

_____

_____

_____

_____

_____

 **©2012 Build Creative Writing Ideas**

Name _____ Date _____

**191.** How many steps do you think it takes for fresh spring vegetables to
make it to your table? What are some ways people might have to work together to send these
healthy treats your way? What could happen if they don't communicate or work well together and
why?

_____

_____

_____

_____

**192.** What are some ways in which the different aspects of nature have to work together to grow
the vegetables in the first place? What are some things that could happen in nature that would
prevent the veggies from growing and why?

_____

_____

_____

_____

                                                              **©2012 Build Creative Writing Ideas**

Name _____ Date _____

**193.** After a lazy winter, what are some ways you can spring into a more active season? What are a few things that could get in your way of being active and productive and why?

_____

_____

_____

_____

**194.** Why is it important to be up and about during the spring? What are some benefits of being outside and moving around? Would you rather be active or lie around during the spring and why?

_____

_____

_____

_____

 **©2012 Build Creative Writing Ideas**

Name _____ Date _____

**195.** Imagine that hundreds of people in your town participated in a huge community garden. What would it be like for so many people to get involved in the planting and why? How would gardening in a big group be different from doing it alone?

_____

_____

_____

_____

**196.** Several months after the planting stage of this huge garden, what would it look like? Describe the many different plants springing up throughout the plot. How would the people involved feel after working together on such a massive agricultural project and why?

_____

_____

_____

_____

Name _____ Date _____

**197.** Imagine that the showers of April went on for seven consecutive days. How would the rain affect your community? How would all of the rain change your daily routine? How would the constant precipitation make you feel and why?

_____

_____

_____

_____

**198.** If it were raining cats and dogs out there, what outfit would you wear to protect yourself? Describe your anti-rain gear from head to toe. What is the most important asset in your outfit and why?

_____

_____

_____

_____

                              **©2012 Build Creative Writing Ideas**

Name _____ Date _____

**199.** Would you consider yourself a flower person? Why or why not?
What do you appreciate the most about flowers and why? What are some aspects of flowers you could do without and why?

_____

_____

_____

_____

**200.** Imagine that you had seasonal allergies during the spring and you started sneezing every time you went outside. How would you spend your season differently from most people? How would you feel if you loved the outdoors but couldn't go outside?

_____

_____

_____

_____

 ©2012 Build Creative Writing Ideas

**Extra Page**

Name _____ Date _____

_____

_____

_____

_____

_____

_____

_____

_____

_____

_____

_____

   ©2012 Build Creative Writing Ideas

## ABOUT THE AUTHOR

Bryan Cohen is a writer, actor and director who grew up in Dresher, Pennsylvania just outside of Philadelphia. He graduated from the University of North Carolina at Chapel Hill with degrees in English and Dramatic Art along with a minor in Creative Writing. His books on writing prompts and writing motivation have sold over 15,000 copies and they include *1,000 Creative Writing Prompts: Ideas for Blogs, Scripts, Stories and More*, *1,000 Character Writing Prompts: Villains, Heroes and Hams for Scripts, Stories and More*, *500 Writing Prompts for Kids: First Grade through Fifth Grade*, *1,000 Character Writing Prompts: Villains, Heroes and Hams for Scripts, Stories and More* and *The Post-College Guide to Happiness*. Cohen continues to produce and perform plays and films in between his books and freelance writing work. He lives in Chicago.

 **©2012 Build Creative Writing Ideas**

23657821R00062

Made in the USA
Lexington, KY
18 June 2013